# *Copyright*

# *Dedication*

To Kiefer, Lar, Larry, and Karl.
I owe you all a drink.

# *Table of Contents*

# *Preface*

## *Why bother learning SQL?*

What's the point of this SQL stuff anyway? Why would anyone bother? Why should YOU bother?

The short answer is that **data is seriously important**. Businesses need data to operate, and they generate tons of it every day. That means they need people who can help organize, access, and interrogate the data they need. Management needs to know whether their widgets are selling and what can be done to sell more of them. Customers need to see what products or services are available. And everyone needs to know if they're meeting their quarterly performance goals.

If you're already doing some data analysis, being able to write SQL yourself will make you faster. You won't have to wait for the SQL guy to set up a query for you, or for the database gal to update your spreadsheet.

For devs, learning SQL will make you more efficient. You'll have a much better idea of what's going on with your data storage layer, you'll be better able to troubleshoot your applications, and you won't get hung up waiting for someone else to fix things.

Best of all, it looks darn good on the resume. **Knowing SQL will make you a more valuable and more efficient employee**.

## *Just how many SQLs are there?*

Like human languages, computer languages can come in a variety of dialects. In the same way that British, Australian, and American English are all slightly different, Oracle, T-SQL, and MySQL are all versions of SQL that are broadly the same - but just a little different.

For this book, we're going to try and keep things as standardized as possible. If you'd like to follow along by running the sample queries yourself, I highly recommend that you download a copy of Microsoft SQL Server Express It's free and 100% compatible with the SQL code in this book.

Be aware that some more advanced commands might look a little different, depending on which flavor of SQL you're working with. I've noted the biggest differences where applicable.

### The audience for this book

Sure, some people learn SQL at school, but many of us end up running in to it while on the job and need a crash course.

Perhaps you've found you need to write a few queries to get the numbers you need to do your job. Maybe you're already a programmer and you find you need to write some SQL queries to support your application. Or it might be that you've suddenly found yourself stuck with some legacy SQL code you now have to support.

The goal of this book is to get you writing *and understanding* SQL queries quickly. And to have fun while we're at it. However you found yourself here, this book will get you up and running with the basics of SQL, so you can get your job done and look brilliant in front of your boss.

Ready to see how it works? Let's get started!

# *Introduction*

## *'hat is SQL, anyway?*

SQL is the language that you use to tell the database what data you want, and how that data is related.

SQL (which stands for Structured Query Language, if you're wondering) can help you get all kinds of insights out of your data. While it *is* a computer language, it's a bit different than, say, C# or Java. With SQL, you're asking the database a question, and the database does all the heavy lifting to get you an answer.

Learning SQL is really just a matter of **figuring out how to ask the right questions.**

## *'hat's a database?*

While SQL is the language, a Relational Database (RDB) is what SQL talks to. A relational database is **a collection of tables that are related to each other**. Tables, in turn, are columns and rows of data.

You can think of a database as a big collection of spreadsheets. That grid of columns and rows, with each cell containing a different piece of data, is actually a pretty good way to picture a SQL table - and the results of SQL queries.

A database is the bucket that holds those tables, just like a workbook holds several spreadsheets.

## *'hat's the big deal with databases?*

Well, spreadsheets can get big and clunky very quickly. Working with SQL is a little like having a turbocharged spreadsheet.

Every business needs to store a lot of data - what employees you have, what products you sell, who your customers are, etc., etc. If all that data was crammed into a single workbook, answering simple questions like 'What products are our top sellers?' would take forever. There's just too much data to sift through.

What's more, it's really tough to do calculations between different spreadsheets in Excel. If you have your sales data in one spreadsheet and your customers in another, you'd have to do a lot of work to figure out which customers ordered what.

Let me give you an example. Here are two spreadsheets:

**Sales**

| Date | CustomerID | OrderID | Item | Quantity |
|---|---|---|---|---|
| 2/5/2016 | 12 | 100 | Widget | |
| 2/5/2016 | 15 | 101 | Thingy | |
| 2/6/2016 | 17 | 102 | Widget | 1 |
| 2/6/2016 | 15 | 103 | Doodad | |
| 2/6/2016 | 14 | 104 | Doodad | |
| 2/6/2016 | 16 | 105 | Doodad | |

**Customers**

| CustomerID | Name | State |
|---|---|---|
| 12 | John Smith | WA |
| 13 | George Washington | DC |
| 14 | Jasmine Cassim | WI |
| 15 | Suzie Fields | OR |
| 16 | Madison Wisconsin | WI |
| 17 | Olivia Bensen | OR |

There's some good data in there, but it's kind of hard to work with. There's no simple, programmatic way in a spreadshee to get answers to questions like...

- What's the name of the customer who purchased the most

Widgets?
- To which state have the most items been shipped?
- Which customer(s) didn't make any purchases in February?

The answers to each of those questions *are* there, but since there's no connection between these two spreadsheets, you'd have to go back and forth between them to find the answer. The more data you put in, the harder it is to get answers back.

That's exactly where **relational databases** come in. A relational database is like a bunch of fancy Excel spreadsheets that **know how to talk to each other**.

In a **relational database**, you can **relate** data from different tables, so you can combine all of the details together. You can tell the computer that the CustomerID in the Sales table is the same as the CustomerID in the Customers table - and then the computer can take it from there.

It does take a little work to learn SQL, but once you get started, you'll find it can save you tons of time and effort in the long run.

Let me show you how! We'll start with the first of our bad SQL jokes.

# Chapter 1

# *SELECT, FROM, and WHERE*

anging in my closet is a t-shirt with this query on it:

> *ELECT \* FROM users WHERE clue > 0*
> *rows returned*

*ude. What is this crap?!*

Yup, it's a SQL joke - and it's actually a fabulous first lesson in reading SQL statements.
Let's break it down, and learn the basics of a SQL query.

*he first bit:* **SELECT \***

SELECT is the first **clause**. A clause is like a sentence within a paragraph. SELECT, FROM, and WHERE are all **clauses**. We'll run into more clauses later in this book, but we're going to stick with the big three for now.

Every query you write has to have at least a SELECT clause - it's the most basic part of a query. The SELECT clause states which **columns** you want to get back. It's the part of the query that says "Show me THIS data."   You can specify either the **names of columns** you want to get from your tables, or you can specify a **calculation**. You could, for example, just write "SELECT 1+2", and SQL would return 3.

What if you don't know which columns you want, or you just want every column in the table? That's what that "*" is for. **SELECT \***      is the same as saying "Show me *all columns* from the table or tables"

If you only want certain columns from the table, you just list each one, separated by a comma. If our "Users" table had columns for UserName and Birthdate, for example, we'd jus need to write them out with a comma in between: "SELECT UserName, Birthdate"

So the **SELECT** clause is the part of the query where you **specify which columns you want to get back**.

### *The second piece:* **FROM users**

Once you've specified the columns you want, you need to tell SQL **where you want to get them FROM**.

This is where you specify the table or tables you're dealing with FROM is the part of the query that says, "…which are in THIS table."

You can name a table just about anything you like - it doesn't matter much to the database. Generally, though, you want t use a name that reflects what the information in the table describes, like Products or Students.

In this example, we're just using a single table, called Users.

### *Last but not least:* **WHERE clue > 0**

Even though we used **SELECT *** to return all the *columns*, we might not want all the *rows* to be returned. **The WHERE clause tells SQL what conditions you want to filter for.**

This is basically the same thing as a filter condition in Excel. WHERE is the part of the query that says, "…And check for THIS stuff."

WHERE clauses can be quite simple, or very complex - it just depends on your needs.

There are several operators you can use in the WHERE clause:

| Operator | Operation |
|---|---|
| = | Equal |
| <> or != | Not Equal |
| > | Greater Than |
| < | Less Than |
| >= | Greater Than or Equal To |
| <= | Less Than or Equal To |
| BETWEEN | Between two values |
| LIKE | Lets you search for a 'fuzzy match'. For example, words that start with the letter A. |
| IN | Allows you to specify a list of values. It's like saying "Equal this OR this OR this." This is a super important one, and you'll use it often. |

## *Translation, please?*

In this joke, WHERE clue > 0 means that we're looking for records in the Users table that have a value in the 'clue' column which is greater than 0. So we can translate it as follows:

"Show me everything from the users table, but give me only those records with a value for 'clue' that is above zero."

So if there are no rows returned for

```
SELECT * FROM users WHERE clue > 0
```

...There must not be any users who have a clue.
Frankly, I'm not surprised.

# Chapter 2

# JOINing tables

*A SQL query walks into a bar, sees two tables, and asks, "May I join you?"*

Yeah, even for a SQL joke, this one's a groaner.

JOINing tables together is the most important thing you can do with SQL. In real life, it's uncommon to write a SQL query that pulls from a single table. Truth is, the data you want is almost never found in just one table.

Why not, you ask? Three simple reasons: **Performance, space, and updates.**

## Performance

Ever tried to open a truly huge spreadsheet on your computer? You know, one of those where the columns go all the way into two letters (AB, AC, AD, etc.), and the scrollbar icon is so tiny, you can barely get your mouse over it? I've crashed computers more than once by trying to open some horrible monster of a spreadsheet sent by a co-worker. I've, uh, never put together a computer-crashing workbook *myself*, of course.

SQL, despite being awesome and powerful, can run into the same sort of trouble. It can handle a lot more than Excel, but packing in too much garbage will still slow things down.

Generally speaking, the 'wider' a table is (i.e. the more columns it has), the slower it's going to be to work with. To a lesser degree, the same is generally true with 'longer' tables - the more rows they have, the slower things go. Breaking the data up into **multiple, smaller tables** so you can work with **only the data you really need** helps to keep things speedy

Of course, SQL can handle volumes of data that would leave a spreadsheet sobbing in the corner. You have to get into some pretty huge tables before things really start breaking down. But that still leaves the second reason to create multiple tables:

### *Space*

Let's say you're putting together a menu for a bar. You're going to sell different kinds of beer and wine. So we'll set up a table called Menu, with columns for DrinkType (Beer or wine), DrinkName, DrinkPrice, and DrinkID.

| DrinkType | DrinkName | DrinkPrice | DrinkID |
|-----------|-----------|------------|---------|
| Beer | Local IPA | 5.00 | 1 |
| Beer | Foreign Porter | 6.00 | 2 |
| Wine | Cabernet | 8.00 | 3 |
| Wine | Merlot | 9.00 | 4 |
| Wine | Chardonnay | 7.00 | 5 |

Because you have more than one kind of beer and more than one kind of wine, that DrinkType field has some repeating values. The words "Beer" and "Wine" are stored multiple times...which is rather inefficient. It might not matter if you have a small menu like this, but what if you had a menu with thousands or even millions of rows? If you had a seriously large wine list, storing the word 'Wine' two thousand times would take up way more space on the hard drive than it should.

If you were working with a university instead of a bar, the problem could be even larger. A university that needed to track the majors of all their students over the years could end up with data overload very quickly. Just imagine recording "Computer Science" a few hundred thousand times for each student in that program - that would take up a lot of space!

## Updates

What's more, **updating records** is difficult with this setup. What if the manager of the bar decided that she wanted to use the word 'Ale' instead of 'Beer' on the menu? If you had a long menu, you'd have to change the text for a whole lot of rows. That means more work for the computer AND more work for you.

There's a better way - use **two tables instead of one**.

Instead of recording the full name of each drink category in our Menu table, we'll **create a separate table called DrinkType**. This table will have one column for DrinkTypeID, and one for DrinkTypeName.

| DrinkTypeID | DrinkTypeName |
|---|---|
| 1 | Beer |
| 2 | Wine |

Now our original Menu table can just store the DrinkTypeID:

| DrinkTypeID | DrinkName | DrinkPrice | DrinkID |
|---|---|---|---|
| 1 | Local IPA | 5.00 | 1 |
| 1 | Foreign Porter | 6.00 | 2 |
| 2 | Cabernet | 8.00 | 3 |
| 2 | Merlot | 9.00 | 4 |
| 2 | Chardonnay | 7.00 | 5 |

As a rule of thumb, **numbers are always more efficient to store in SQL than text** - so we're already taking up a lot less space by using a numeric ID for our DrinkType instead of spelling it out. And now, if we want to change "Beer" to "Ale", we only have to update **a single field in our DrinkType table**. The Menu table can remain just the way i is!

This process of splitting tables up - so you make things faster, less repetitive, and smarter - is called **normalization**.

Now, normalization is kind of a fuzzy thing. You can break up your data a little bit or a lot - there's no one, single way to normalize your tables. Depending on what you're going to use your database for, you may want to make the tables more or less normalized.

There are a lot of theories out there over just how much normalization is right for each situation, and everyone's got their own pet theory. If you want to sound smart - or if you want to annoy a database administrator - ask them about their approach to normalization in your company's database

For now, though, just bear in mind that **storing too much duplicate data slows things down**, and **all databases wil be normalized to some degree**.

## *ay I Join You?*

Alright, let's get inside that joke now, and find out how you actually JOIN tables together.

First of all, imagine that you've just walked into a bar, and you see two literal wooden tables in front of you. On the right-hand table, someone has left a copy of the menu. It looks like a group has just stepped away from the left-hand table, leaving a glass of beer and three different glasses of wine behind.

It's a pretty good bet that the drinks on the left table are listed in the menu on the right table - in other words, the two tables are **related**. So if these were SQL tables, there should be some way to **link the data in each table together.**

Let's set up these tables in our database. If you'd like to follow along (and really, you should - this will make a lot more sense when you run a few queries yourself), you can open a new query window and run the following script on your computer:

```
CREATE DATABASE SQL_Smile
GO
```

```
USE SQL_Smile
GO

CREATE TABLE Menu
(
DrinkTypeID INT
,DrinkName VARCHAR(50)
,DrinkPrice MONEY
,DrinkID INT)
GO

INSERT INTO Menu (DrinkTypeID,
DrinkName, DrinkPrice, DrinkID)
    VALUES (1,'Local IPA',5,1),
    (1,'Foreign Porter',6,2),
    (2,'Cabernet',8,3),
    (2,'Merlot',9,4),
    (2,'Chardonnay',7,5)
GO

CREATE TABLE DrinkOrders
(
OrderDate DATE
,OrderID VARCHAR(50)
,DrinkID INT
)
GO

INSERT INTO DrinkOrders
(OrderDate, OrderID, DrinkID)
    VALUES ('2/5/2016',1,2),
    ('2/5/2016',1,5),
    ('2/5/2016',1,4),
    ('2/5/2016',1,3)
GO
```

Don't worry about figuring out all the details of this script just
yet. It just sets up a sample database and two tables, so we

can run some of these examples.

Since we're going to be working with these tables for the first
time, we should use that SELECT * command we heard
about in the first joke to see what kind of data we'll be
working with.

Let's start with the right-hand table, which is called Menu. Our
query will look like this:

```
SELECT *
FROM Menu
```

esults:

| rinkTypeID | DrinkName | DrinkPrice | DrinkID |
|---|---|---|---|
| 1 | Local IPA | 5.00 | 1 |
| 1 | Foreign Porter | 6.00 | 2 |
| 2 | Cabernet | 8.00 | 3 |
| 2 | Merlot | 9.00 | 4 |
| 2 | Chardonnay | 7.00 | 5 |

This looks just like the Menu table we reviewed earlier - we can
see the DrinkType, DrinkName, DrinkPrice, and DrinkID for
each item on the menu.

Let's check out the left-hand table, called **DrinkOrders,** next.
The query is:

```
SELECT *
FROM DrinkOrders
```

esults:

| rderDate | OrderID | DrinkID |
|---|---|---|
| 2/5/2016 | 1 | 2 |
| 2/5/2016 | 1 | 5 |
| 2/5/2016 | 1 | 4 |
| 2/5/2016 | 1 | 3 |

This time, we get the columns OrderDate, OrderID, and DrinkID.

It looks like this DrinkOrders table can tell you what was ordere and when, but unless you've memorized the menu, just seeing that DrinkID doesn't tell you much. Was DrinkID 4 th Cabernet or the Merlot?

It would be useful to get the DrinkName field in here. **That's where JOINing tables comes in**. Both Menu and DrinkOrders have a **DrinkID** column, so we can use that information to relate the two tables together.

*"Do you have a significant other right now?" "Nah, I'll leav relations to the databases."*

To write a query that JOINs both tables together, we'll need to tell SQL two things: **which tables we're working with**, anc **on which column or columns the data is related**. Here's what that would look like:

```
SELECT *
FROM DrinkOrders
JOIN Menu
  ON DrinkOrders.DrinkID =
Menu.DrinkID
```

Pretty straightforward, right? We've told SQL which tables we'r using (in our case, DrinkOrders and Menu), and then which columns inside those tables (DrinkOrders.DrinkID and Menu.DrinkID) can be used to relate the data.

Notice that the table names are used when specifying which columns to JOIN on. It doesn't matter what order you put them in (DrinkOrders.DrinkID = Menu.DrinkID is the same a Menu.DrinkID = DrinkOrders.DrinkID), but you do need to specify the table names, or else SQL won't know which DrinkID column you're talking about. Computers aren't very imaginative.

If we run this query, we'll get all of the columns from both table

That gives us the information we're looking for...but it also gives us a lot of extra data we don't really need.

≥sults:

| rderDate | OrderID | DrinkID | DrinkTypeID | DrinkName | DrinkPrice | DrinkID |
|---|---|---|---|---|---|---|
| 2/5/2016 | 1 | 2 | 1 | Foreign Porter | 6.00 | 2 |
| 2/5/2016 | 1 | 3 | 2 | Cabernet | 8.00 | 3 |
| 2/5/2016 | 1 | 4 | 2 | Merlot | 9.00 | 4 |
| 2/5/2016 | 1 | 5 | 2 | Chardonnay | 7.00 | 5 |

We can even see two DrinkID columns, since that field is present in both tables. That really doesn't add anything, so let's get rid of the extra columns. Instead of using SELECT *, we can specify only those columns we actually want. Let's try this:

```
SELECT OrderDate, OrderID,
rinkID, DrinkName, DrinkPrice
FROM DrinkOrders
JOIN Menu
ON DrinkOrders.DrinkID =
enu.DrinkID
```

Whoops, there's a problem! If you try and run that query, you're going to get an error that says something like, *Ambiguous column name 'DrinkID'.*

The problem is the computer's lack of imagination again. Since DrinkID shows up in both tables, **SQL doesn't know which table you'd like to pull that column from**.

Just like we did in the ON clause, you need to **specify the name of the table before the column name**, so SQL knows which DrinkID you're talking about. Since the values are the same in each table, it doesn't *really* matter whether we write Menu.DrinkID, or DrinkOrders.DrinkID, but we still have to tell the computer which one we want.

To make things simple, I like to use whichever table comes firs in the FROM clause. So, since DrinkOrders is listed first in the FROM clause, I'll use DrinkOrders.DrinkID. Let's re-writ our query with that table name in our SELECT statement:

```
        SELECT OrderDate, OrderID,
DrinkOrders.DrinkID, DrinkName,
DrinkPrice
        FROM DrinkOrders
        JOIN Menu
        ON DrinkOrders.DrinkID =
Menu.DrinkID
```

Now, our query works!

Results:

| OrderDate | OrderID | DrinkID | DrinkName | DrinkPrice |
|-----------|---------|---------|-----------|------------|
| 2/5/2016 | 1 | 2 | Foreign Porter | 6.00 |
| 2/5/2016 | 1 | 3 | Cabernet | 8.00 |
| 2/5/2016 | 1 | 4 | Merlot | 9.00 |
| 2/5/2016 | 1 | 5 | Chardonnay | 7.00 |

While it's only necessary to specify the table name when a column name is not unique, you *can* specify the table name for each column if you'd like. In fact, it's not a bad idea to write all of your SQL queries with the table name specified for each column, because it makes it a lot easier for other people reading your query to see what you're doing.

Of course, it can make your query look a lot longer. Here's our query with all the table names specified:

```
    SELECT DrinkOrders.OrderDate,
rinkOrders.OrderID,
rinkOrders.DrinkID, Menu.DrinkName,
enu.DrinkPrice
    FROM DrinkOrders
    JOIN Menu
    ON DrinkOrders.DrinkID =
enu.DrinkID
```

Man, that's kind of hard to look at! The query is suddenly a lot longer. There's a quick trick for shortening that, though: a **table alias.** By giving each table a short nickname, the query becomes a lot more readable:

```
    SELECT DO.OrderDate, DO.OrderID,
.DrinkID, M.DrinkName, M.DrinkPrice
    FROM DrinkOrders AS DO
    JOIN Menu AS M
    ON DO.DrinkID = M.DrinkID
```

Ahh, that's much better. In fact, you can shorten things up even more by removing the keyword 'AS' next to your table name:

```
    SELECT DO.OrderDate, DO.OrderID,
.DrinkID, M.DrinkName, M.DrinkPrice
    FROM DrinkOrders DO
    JOIN Menu M
    ON DO.DrinkID = M.DrinkID
```

Our results from this query still look the same as before, but now it's easier for anyone else who looks at this query to figure out where each column comes from.

Bear in mind that once you assign a table alias, you have to us it consistently throughout your query. SQL will now think of the Menu table as 'M', and any reference to 'Menu' will go right over its head.

If we try to mix things up like this:

```
    SELECT DO.OrderDate, DO.OrderID,
DO.DrinkID, Menu.DrinkName,
M.DrinkPrice
    FROM DrinkOrders DO
    JOIN Menu M
    ON DO.DrinkID = M.DrinkID
```

…We'll get an error saying that *The multi-part identifier "Menu.DrinkName" could not be bound.* Always be consistent with table names in your query.

## Different Ways of JOINing the Party - LEFT, RIGHT, INNER, OUTER

Alright, let's switch things up a bit and see how different kinds JOINs give you different results in your SQL query.

In our hypothetical bar, someone has just come in and left a bottle of water on the left table. Bottled water isn't on the menu! What will happen now if we re-run our query?

First, let's put that bottle of water on the table. If you're followin along, you can run this script to add the water bottle to you table:

```
    USE SQL_Smile
    GO

    INSERT INTO DrinkOrders
    VALUES ('2/5/2016',1,6);
```

31

You should see a message that says something like *(1 row(s) affected)*.

Now, let's run our query and see what happens:

```
SELECT DO.OrderDate, DO.OrderID,
O.DrinkID, M.DrinkName, M.DrinkPrice
FROM DrinkOrders DO
JOIN Menu M
ON DO.DrinkID = M.DrinkID
```

esults:

| rderDate | OrderID | DrinkID | DrinkName | DrinkPrice |
|---|---|---|---|---|
| 2/5/2016 | 1 | 2 | Foreign Porter | 6.00 |
| 2/5/2016 | 1 | 3 | Cabernet | 8.00 |
| 2/5/2016 | 1 | 4 | Merlot | 9.00 |
| 2/5/2016 | 1 | 5 | Chardonnay | 7.00 |

The answer is…well, nothing happens. Our results look exactly the same. But we know that the bottle of water is there - so, what gives?

The culprit here is the **way we phrased our JOIN**. It turns out that JOIN comes in a few different flavors:

- INNER JOIN
- LEFT OUTER JOIN
- RIGHT OUTER JOIN
- FULL OUTER JOIN
- CROSS JOIN

What's the difference? Each of these different kinds of JOINs tells SQL whether you want **records that don't exist in one or the other table**.

Let's take these JOINs one at a time, and see how they change our query's results.

## *INNER JOIN*

An INNER JOIN returns **ONLY those results that are contained in BOTH tables**. You don't actually have to use the word "inner" - if you just use the word JOIN, as we did ir our first queries, then SQL will perform an INNER JOIN.

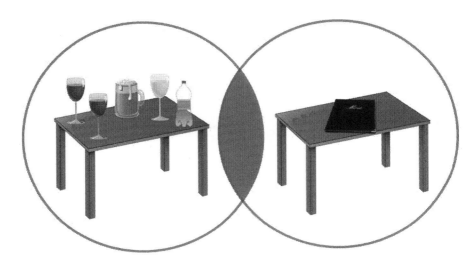

This explains why our results didn't change when someone left a bottle of water on the left table. When we use an INNER JOIN, SQL is only going to return records that match in both places - the overlapping area of the Venn diagram. Since there's no entry on the menu for bottled water, we won't see any records for the water.

## *LEFT OUTER JOIN and RIGHT OUTER JOIN*

LEFT or RIGHT OUTER JOINS are used when you'd like to ge **ALL the records from one table AND all the records tha match in another table**.

Just like you can leave the word INNER off of the INNER JOIN you don't have to specify the word OUTER - just typing LEFT JOIN or RIGHT JOIN will work.

Here's what the Left and Right joins look like with our tables.

First, the LEFT OUTER JOIN:

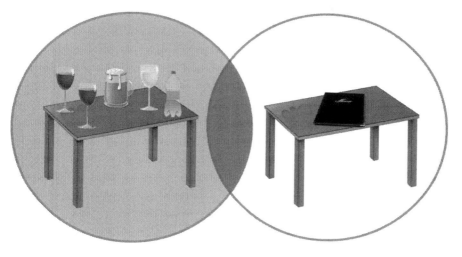

And the RIGHT OUTER JOIN:

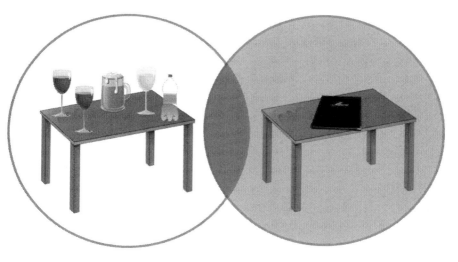

Let's try a LEFT JOIN on our tables first:

```
SELECT DO.OrderDate, DO.OrderID,
DO.DrinkID, M.DrinkName, M.DrinkPrice
    FROM DrinkOrders DO
    LEFT JOIN Menu M
    ON DO.DrinkID = M.DrinkID
```

Results:

| OrderDate | OrderID | DrinkID | DrinkName | DrinkPrice |
|-----------|---------|---------|-----------|------------|
| 2/5/2016 | 1 | 2 | Foreign Porter | 6.00 |
| 2/5/2016 | 1 | 5 | Chardonnay | 7.00 |
| 2/5/2016 | 1 | 4 | Merlot | 9.00 |
| 2/5/2016 | 1 | 3 | Cabernet | 8.00 |
| 2/5/2016 | 1 | 6 | NULL | NULL |

Now, we get all the same results we had before, PLUS an extra row. Hey, that's the bottled water!

The water is showing up because we've asked SQL for *all* **values from the DrinkOrders table** *and* **matching values from the Menu table.**

You can see that the new row has values for OrderDate, OrderID, and DrinkID, because those fields come from the DrinkOrders table where the bottle of water exists. But since bottled water doesn't exist in the menu, there's no data for the DrinkName and DrinkPrice fields.

What's the difference between LEFT and RIGHT OUTER JOINS? It's literally just the placement of the tables. We could get exactly the same results as above if we re-arranged our FROM statement to list the Menu table **first** and the DrinkOrders table **second**, and then used a **RIGHT JOIN**, like this:

```
SELECT DO.OrderDate, DO.OrderID,
O.DrinkID, M.DrinkName, M.DrinkPrice
FROM Menu M
RIGHT JOIN DrinkOrders DO
ON DO.DrinkID = M.DrinkID
```

Since we're still pulling **all values from the DrinkOrders table and matching values from the Menu table**, the result set stays exactly the same.

esults:

| rderDate | OrderID | DrinkID | DrinkName | DrinkPrice |
|---|---|---|---|---|
| 2/5/2016 | 1 | 2 | Foreign Porter | 6.00 |
| 2/5/2016 | 1 | 5 | Chardonnay | 7.00 |
| 2/5/2016 | 1 | 4 | Merlot | 9.00 |
| 2/5/2016 | 1 | 3 | Cabernet | 8.00 |
| 2/5/2016 | 1 | 6 | NULL | NULL |

In practice, people hardly ever use the RIGHT JOIN. For those of us who read our native language left to right, it makes sense to arrange our tables from left to right, too.

It can be difficult to keep track of which table is where if you mix LEFT and RIGHT JOINs in your query, so it's usually simpler to arrange everything so you only use LEFT JOINs.

There's one more thing to note here: the word "NULL" that's returned for DrinkName and DrinkPrice in the last record. **A NULL value is not the same as a zero**, and it's **not the same as 'nothing'** - it means '**Unknown Value**'. SQL is just throwing up its hands here and saying it doesn't have a clue.

Because the value is unknown, a NULL isn't equal to anything else. NULLs are like Chuck Norris - nothing can compare!

## FULL OUTER JOIN

A FULL OUTER JOIN returns rows from both tables **regardless of whether either matches anything in the other table.** It's like taking all the unique results of a LEFT JOIN and of a RIGHT JOIN, together. Or to put it another way, a FULL OUTER JOIN just asks SQL to give you everything, and match it up wherever it can.

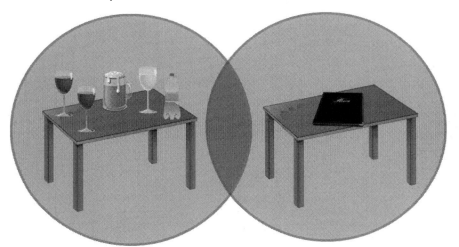

We can use a FULL OUTER JOIN to see which items (like that bottled water) are in the DrinkOrders table and not the Menu table, and at the same time which items are on the menu, but have not been ordered.

As with other JOINs, SQL lets you leave out the 'OUTER' keyword if you're feeling lazy:

```
SELECT DO.OrderDate, DO.OrderID,
DO.DrinkID, M.DrinkName, M.DrinkPrice
FROM Menu M
FULL JOIN DrinkOrders DO
ON DO.DrinkID = M.DrinkID
```

Results:

| OrderDate | OrderID | DrinkID | DrinkName | DrinkPrice |
|-----------|---------|---------|-----------|------------|
| NULL | NULL | NULL | Local IPA | 5.00 |

| 2/5/2016 | 1 | 2 | Foreign Porter | 6.00 |
| 2/5/2016 | 1 | 3 | Cabernet | 8.00 |
| 2/5/2016 | 1 | 4 | Merlot | 9.00 |
| 2/5/2016 | 1 | 5 | Chardonnay | 7.00 |
| 2/5/2016 | 1 | 6 | NULL | NULL |

Now our result set includes that bottled water, the drinks that were ordered off the menu, AND a local beer that's on the menu, but which no one has ordered yet.

## CROSS JOIN

CROSS JOINs aren't used very often, and there is a good reason to be careful with them - the result set you get back can be **huge**. A CROSS JOIN returns the **rows in the first table *multiplied* by the rows in the second table.**

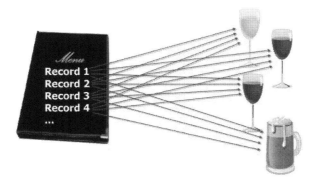

Since you're using every row, you don't have to specify which columns you're joining on when using a CROSS JOIN, only the two table names. You can, however, restrict your records by using a WHERE clause.

**Be careful using this join** - you can quickly end up with a huge number of records if you use a CROSS JOIN on a pair of moderately large tables. Even with our teeny tiny tables, if we try a cross join as in this query:

```
SELECT *
FROM Menu
CROSS JOIN DrinkOrders
```

...You'll get 25 rows back.

CROSS JOINs can let you produce some pretty neat SQL tricks, but for now, most of your work will probably be done with INNER JOINS and LEFT (or RIGHT) OUTER JOINs.

# Chapter 3

# Aggregate Functions and GROUP BY

```
SELECT COUNT(Flips) AS NumberOfFlipsGiven
    FROM Employee
    WHERE Given = 1
```

Results:

| NumberOfFlipsGiven |
| --- |
| 0 |

**Aggregate functions** are the bread and butter of analysis, and you'll find yourself using these a lot right from the start. Whenever you have a quantity or a price for something, you'll need an aggregate function to add it all up.

The five aggregate functions used most often are: COUNT(), SUM(), AVG(), MIN(), and MAX(). For each of these functions, the calculation you want to make is entered in parentheses right after the keyword. So for example, if you want to count how many flips were given, you could use the following query:

```
SELECT COUNT(Flips) AS NumberOfFlipsGiven
FROM Employee
WHERE Given = 1
```

Of course, we'd expect to see 0 Rows Returned.

Note that we've got an alias happening here: *COUNT(Flips) AS NumberOfFlipsGiven*.

Instead of renaming a *table*, we're now using an alias to rename a *column* within the SELECT statement.

42

Why? Well, when you aggregate a column, SQL doesn't know what to call it anymore. Just because the original column in our joke query was called 'Flips', **that doesn't mean that it's a good description of the number we're going to ge after performing a calculation with that data.** So we nee to tell SQL what to call the resulting column.

When aliasing a column, make sure you come up with a colum name that describes the data - NumberOfFlipsGiven is fine but CountOfFlips or FlipCount would also work.

Let's go over each of the five major aggregate functions, and see how we can use them with our sample bar data.

### SUM()

SUM() adds all the values together. Let's JOIN our Men and DrinkOrders table together and look at the SUM cost of the drinks ordered:

```
SELECT DO.OrderID, SUM(M.DrinkPrice) AS
TotalPriceSold
    FROM DrinkOrders DO
    INNER JOIN Menu M
    ON DO.DrinkID = M.DrinkID
```

D'oh! When we try to run this query, we get an error:

Msg 8120, Level 16, State 1, Line 1
Column 'DrinkOrders.OrderID' is invalid in the select list because it is not contained in either an aggregate function or the GROUP BY clause.

Wow. What the heck does that mean?

Well, it looks like it's time to meet another SQL clause - GROU **BY**.

When you use an aggregate function, you need to decide how

you want to break the numbers out. If you think about it, this does make a lot of sense - **you are GROUPing the numbers into different buckets**.

Like the error message says, once you have an aggregate function, everything else in your SELECT list has to either be included in another aggregate or in the GROUP BY clause.

In our case, because we want to see the **total amount spent for each OrderID**, we want to **GROUP the DrinkPrice values BY each OrderID**. Here's how that would look:

```
SELECT DO.OrderID, SUM(M.DrinkPrice) AS
otalPriceSold
FROM DrinkOrders DO
INNER JOIN Menu M
ON DO.DrinkID = M.DrinkID
GROUP BY DO.OrderID
```

That did the trick!

esults:

| rderID | TotalPriceSold |
|---|---|
| 1 | 30.00 |

### COUNT(), COUNT(*), and COUNT(DISTINCT)

Just like it says on the tin, the COUNT() function counts how many records there are.

In the same way you can use SELECT * to get all records from a table, you can use COUNT(*) to see how many rows a table has. Here's an example:

```
SELECT COUNT(*) AS MenuRowCount
FROM Menu
```

Results:

| MenuRowCount |
|---|
| 5 |

This is a great way to check how large a table is, which is especially useful when you're looking at a new table for the first time. If you find that you're dealing with a big table with whole lot of records, you know that you'll probably want to add some filtering to the WHERE clause of your query so you don't get swamped with too many results.

Note that **we didn't use a GROUP BY clause here**. Since we're only getting one column back, and therefore **all of ou columns are included in an aggregate function**, we don need to.

COUNT() can also be used to answer some useful business questions. To find out how many drinks are on the menu, fo example, you can use:

```
SELECT COUNT(DrinkID) AS
Number_Of_Drinks_Offered
FROM Menu
```

esults:

| umber_Of_Drinks_Offered |
|---|
| 5 |

With that info, you might try the following to find out how many orders have been placed using the same function:

```
SELECT COUNT(OrderID) AS Order_Count
FROM DrinkOrders
```

esults:

| rder_Count |
|---|
| 5 |

...Wait. We know there's only been one order so far. Why would we get a result of 5?

It's because we have five rows in that table - one record for each drink ordered. Each row has the same OrderID, but the COUNT() function doesn't care about that - it counts each row separately.

| rderDate | OrderID | DrinkID |
|---|---|---|
| 2/5/2016 | 1 | 2 |
| 2/5/2016 | 1 | 5 |
| 2/5/2016 | 1 | 4 |
| 2/5/2016 | 1 | 3 |
| 2/5/2016 | 1 | 6 |

There's a fix for that, though! If we want to see how many **unique** order IDs we have, we can use COUNT(DISTINCT) instead:

```
SELECT COUNT(DISTINCT OrderID) AS Order_Count
FROM DrinkOrders
```

esults:

| rder_Count |
|---|
| 1 |

There we go!

A word of caution - You can use COUNT(DISTINCT) even in those cases where you don't have duplicate values. For example, using either COUNT(DrinkID) or COUNT(DISTINCT DrinkID) against our Menu table will bo return the correct value of 5:

```
SELECT COUNT(DrinkID) AS
Number_Of_Drinks_Offered
    FROM Menu
```

Results:

| Number_Of_Drinks_Offered |
|---|
| 5 |

But keep in mind that using COUNT(DISTINCT) takes more computing power than a regular COUNT(). It's sloppy programming to use COUNT(DISTINCT) in places where you don't actually need it. So be kind to your SQL server, and make sure you're using the right COUNT().

# *IN()*

The function MIN() returns the lowest value for the specified column or calculation. To find the least expensive drink:

```
SELECT MIN(DrinkPrice) AS Cheapest_Drink_Price
FROM Menu
```

esults:

| heapest_Drink_Price |
| --- |
| 5.00 |

# *AX()*

Yup, you guessed it - MAX() returns the highest value for the specified column or calculation. So, to find the most expensive drink:

```
SELECT MAX(DrinkPrice) AS
ost_Expensive_Drink_Price
FROM Menu
```

esults:

| ost_Expensive_Drink_Price |
| --- |
| 9.00 |

## AVG()

Average, abbreviated AVG() in SQL, returns the mathematical mean of the specified column or calculation. If it's been a while since your last math class (it sure has been for me), the mean is what you usually think of when someone says 'average' - the sum of all values divided by the number of values.

To find the average price of a drink on our menu:

```
SELECT AVG(DrinkPrice) AS Average_Drink_Pri
FROM Menu
```

Results:

| Average_Drink_Price |
|---|
| 7.00 |

Man, is it just me, or have drinks gotten expensive these days

## Calculations

There's one more useful thing you can do with aggregate functions. Instead of just adding up a single column, you can also enter a **calculation**. Let's say we want to look at how much our customers would have spent if we hiked the prices of each drink by a dollar:

```
SELECT DO.OrderID, SUM(M.DrinkPrice+1) AS
riceIncreaseTotalSold
    FROM DrinkOrders DO
    INNER JOIN Menu M
    ON DO.DrinkID = M.DrinkID
    GROUP BY DO.OrderID
```

esults:

| rderID | PriceIncreaseTotalSold |
|--------|------------------------|
| 1      | 34.00                  |

All aggregate functions - not just SUM() - can take a calculation like this. You can get as complicated as you want in your calculations, so get creative!

# Chapter 4

# TOP and ORDER BY

```
SELECT TOP 1 Date_Prospect
FROM BarAttendees
WHERE Attached = 'FALSE'
ORDER BY BloodAlcoholContent DESC
```

Like peanut butter and jelly, the TOP and ORDER BY functions
go together beautifully. While you can use each function
separately, they're even more powerful when their powers
are combined.

## TOP

The **TOP** function **returns the first N records**. You can specify
any number, so it's possible to return the top 1, top 10, or top
1,000 rows - whatever you need.

While TOP returns the first records, though, what SQL
considers "first" can seem pretty random. **By default, query
results don't come back in any particular order.** So,
almost any time you use TOP, you will also need…

## ORDER BY

**ORDER BY sorts the values of your result set**. As with
aggregate functions, you can use either a column name *or* a
calculation to tell SQL how you want the records to be
sorted, so it's incredibly flexible. You can also specify
whether the results should be sorted in ascending order
(using the keyword ASC), or descending order (using the
keyword DESC).

## TOP 1 vs. MIN() and MAX() - What's The Difference?

As we learned in the last chapter, MIN() and MAX() can help you get the highest or lowest value. So why would you eve▪ need to use TOP 1 in your SELECT statement?

Well, there's one important difference: MIN() and MAX() work ▪ the column or calculation specified. That means MIN() and MAX() answer the question, **"What is the smallest (or biggest) value found for each record?"**

TOP 1, on the other hand, answers the question, **"What's the first record you get back?"**

Here, it'll make more sense with an example. In the last chapter, we used MIN() to find the cheapest drink:

```
SELECT MIN(DrinkPrice) AS Cheapest_Drink_Pri
FROM Menu
```

Results:

| Cheapest_Drink_Price |
|---|
| 5.00 |

That gives us the correct value, but what if we wanted to get some more information, like the name and ID of the drink? MIN() won't work here:

```
SELECT MIN(DrinkPrice) AS MinDrinkPrice,
DrinkName, DrinkID
    FROM Menu
    GROUP BY DrinkName, DrinkID
```

esults:

| inDrinkPrice | DrinkName | DrinkID |
|---:|---|---:|
| 5.00 | Local IPA | 1 |
| 6.00 | Foreign Porter | 2 |
| 8.00 | Cabernet | 3 |
| 9.00 | Merlot | 4 |
| 7.00 | Chardonnay | 5 |

Why do we have so many records, when we just wanted to see the cheapest drink? Well, since MIN() answers the question, "What is the smallest value for each record?", we end up with **the minimum price for every drink in the Menu table**. Not what we're looking for at all.

Here's where TOP and ORDER BY can help! Let's change that query to use TOP instead, and use ORDER BY to sort our drinks by price:

```
SELECT TOP 1 DrinkName, DrinkID, DrinkPrice AS
ieapest_Drink_Price
FROM Menu
ORDER BY DrinkPrice
```

esults:

| inkName | DrinkID | Cheapest_Drink_Price |
|---|---:|---:|
| cal IPA | 1 | 5.00 |

There we go - TOP handled the question we were *really* asking, which was "**What's the first record you get back if you sort for the smallest DrinkPrice amount?**"

If you were to run the query without the TOP clause…

```
SELECT DrinkName, DrinkID, DrinkPrice AS
ieapest_Drink_Price
FROM Menu
ORDER BY DrinkPrice
```

...You'd get these results:

| DrinkName | DrinkID | Cheapest_Drink_Price |
|-----------|---------|----------------------|
| Local IPA | 1 | 5.00 |
| Foreign Porter | 2 | 6.00 |
| Chardonnay | 5 | 7.00 |
| Cabernet | 3 | 8.00 |
| Merlot | 4 | 9.00 |

Just like we wanted, the ORDER BY clause has arranged thing so the cheapest drink comes on top. So the TOP clause jus restricts this result set to the first row returned, and ignores all the other records.

### TOP and Largest Values

Just like MIN() and MAX() are mirror images of each other, you might wonder if TOP has a matching function that gives you the *last* X records. Well, it actually doesn't - but that's where ORDER BY comes in.

To get the lowest price, we specified that we wanted to ORDER BY DrinkPrice, but we didn't say whether we wanted to sort in ascending or descending order. This worked because **by default, SQL arranges data in an ascending order**, so you see the smallest numbers first. If we want to see the highes numbers first, we need to sort the data in *descending* order. Here's how we can use the TOP function to get the highest price instead:

```
    SELECT TOP 1 DrinkName, DrinkID, DrinkPrice /
Most_Expensive_Drink_Price
    FROM Menu
    ORDER BY DrinkPrice DESC
```

ɘsults:

| rinkName | DrinkID | Most_Expensive_Drink_Price |
|---|---|---|
| erlot | 4 | 9.00 |

## ake Your Own Top 10 List

Want to get more than just one top record? Just use TOP 10, TOP 100, or whatever number you'd like. For example, we can check out the top 3 priciest drinks with the following:

```
SELECT TOP 3 DrinkName, DrinkID, DrinkPrice
FROM Menu
ORDER BY DrinkPrice DESC
```

ɘsults:

| rinkName | DrinkID | DrinkPrice |
|---|---|---|
| erlot | 4 | 9.00 |
| abernet | 3 | 8.00 |
| 1ardonnay | 5 | 7.00 |

## ɘsting Out Tables With TOP

The TOP function is great for one more trick - getting a glimpse at the data in an unfamiliar table. If a table is especially large, running a regular SELECT * query can take a long time and leave you flooded with way more data than you need.

So, to get a quick look at a table, you can add TOP to your query:

```
SELECT TOP 4 *
FROM DrinkOrders
```

Results:

| OrderDate | OrderID | DrinkID |
|-----------|---------|---------|
| 2/5/2016 | 1 | 2 |
| 2/5/2016 | 1 | 5 |
| 2/5/2016 | 1 | 4 |
| 2/5/2016 | 1 | 3 |

**It's good to get into the habit of taking a quick look at any new table with TOP.** With a better idea of what the data looks like, you'll be able to write much more successful queries.

## Life's Different in Oracle PL/SQL

Just when you thought you were getting this TOP thing down, I'm afraid I have to throw a wrench into the works. Each implementation of SQL handles the idea of TOP differently, and **Oracle's edition of SQL does not have the TOP function.** In fact, Oracle's approach to this problem is very different than other flavors of SQL.

Instead of using the TOP function, **you can get the top N records by using Oracle's Rownum function in the WHERE clause**.

How does it work? Well, let's start with a quick example. Let's say we want to get back the **top three least expensive drinks**. First, let's set up a query that returns all the drinks and sorts them in order from lowest to highest price:

```
SELECT DrinkName, DrinkID, DrinkPrice
FROM Menu
ORDER BY DrinkPrice ASC
```

Nice and short, right? Now that we have our data coming back in the right order, we need to do three things:

- **Wrap this query in parentheses**, so it will be executed first
- **Add a WHERE clause that filters for Rownum**, so we can get the three records we want
- **Add another ORDER BY clause that sorts on Rownum**, so we can see the top three records in order

Here's what it looks like all put together:

```
SELECT *
FROM
      (
          SELECT DrinkName, DrinkID, DrinkPrice
          FROM Menu
          ORDER BY DrinkPrice ASC
      )
WHERE Rownum <=3
ORDER BY Rownum
```

If you remember, our Menu table doesn't have a column called "Rownum" - so where is it coming from? **Rownum is not a real column** - it's a pseudo-column, a bit of metadata that Oracle generates on the fly while it processes your query. That means that **there aren't any values for Rownum until your query is already running**.

It sounds like a Catch-22 situation, doesn't it? You can't figure out your top records until you run a query, so how are you supposed to write a query to get the top records?

Well, the answer is that you need *two* queries. Query one is outside those parentheses, and query two is inside:

```
SELECT *
FROM
        (
        SELECT DrinkName, DrinkID, DrinkPrice
        FROM Menu
        ORDER BY DrinkPrice ASC
        )
WHERE Rownum <=3
ORDER BY Rownum
```

We're asking Oracle SQL to **first sort all the records in our Menu table by DrinkPrice**. Then we ask it to **give us the first three records from those results** (that's the "WHER Rownum <=3" part), and finally, we ask it to **show us thos three records in order from 1 to 3** (the "ORDER BY Rownum" part).

So, when you want to get the Top N records in Oracle, you ne to:
- Write a query for the data you want, sorted the way you wa it
- Wrap the query in parentheses
- Add a WHERE clause that filters for Rownum
- Add an ORDER BY clause that sorts on Rownum

It's a bit more complicated than the TOP function, but it works. In fact, what we've just written here is a kind of **subquery**. What's a subquery? I'm glad you asked - let's hop into the next chapter and talk about it!

# Chapter 5

# Subqueries

```
SELECT *
FROM World
WHERE Location NOT IN
    (SELECT Location
    FROM World
    WHERE Lightning_ Count >=1)
```

*Lightning never strikes the same place twice!*

A **subquery**, sometimes called a nested or inner query, is **a query within a query**. Subqueries are complete and entire queries in and of themselves, but they happen to be living inside a pair of parentheses within a larger, outer query

Just like in algebra, where calculations inside parentheses are done first, **SQL calculates subqueries first and the outer query last**.

If you've got a programming background, you can think of subqueries as *subroutines.*

## *ummarizing Subqueries*

They sound complicated, but as we saw in our Oracle example with Rownum, subqueries are actually both useful and simple!

Let's go through a few more examples. But first, let's put some new records in our DrinkOrders table, and add the DrinkType table we outlined in chapter 2. If you're following along, open a query window and run the following script:

```
USE SQL_Smile
GO

CREATE TABLE DrinkType
(
DrinkTypeID INT
,DrinkTypeName VARCHAR(50)
)
GO

INSERT INTO DrinkType (DrinkTypeID,
DrinkTypeName)
    VALUES (1,'Beer'),
    (2,'Wine')
GO

INSERT INTO DrinkOrders (OrderDate, OrderID,
DrinkID)
    VALUES ('2016-02-05', 2, 1),
    ('2016-02-05', 2, 2),
    ('2016-02-05', 2, 2),
    ('2016-02-05', 2, 2),
    ('2016-02-05', 2, 3),
    ('2016-02-05', 2, 4),
    ('2016-02-05', 2, 5),
    ('2016-02-05', 2, 5),
    ('2016-02-05', 2, 4),
    ('2016-02-05', 2, 2),
    ('2016-02-05', 2, 5),
    ('2016-02-05', 2, 4);
```

You should see a couple of messages like '(2 row(s) affected)' and '(12 row(s) affected)'

Now that we have a few new orders, it would be great to know which drinks are selling well. Let's start with the wines. Which varieties are the customers purchasing the most?

We have a few different wines on the menu, so let's grab their DrinkNames using a query:

```
SELECT Menu.DrinkID, Menu.DrinkName
FROM Menu
JOIN DrinkType
ON Menu.DrinkTypeID = DrinkType.DrinkTypeID
WHERE  DrinkType.DrinkTypeName = 'Wine'
```

ɘsults:

| ʻinkID | DrinkName |
|---|---|
| 3 | Cabernet |
| 4 | Merlot |
| 5 | Chardonnay |

With that list of wine names, we could just type them all into a WHERE clause:

```
SELECT COUNT(DrinkOrders.DrinkID) AS
ɪmDrinksSold, Menu.DrinkName
FROM DrinkOrders
JOIN Menu ON DrinkOrders.DrinkID =
ɘnu.DrinkID
WHERE Menu.DrinkName IN
Cabernet','Chardonnay','Merlot')
GROUP BY Menu.DrinkName
```

ɘsults:

| ɪmDrinksSold | DrinkName |
|---|---|
| 2 | Cabernet |
| 4 | Chardonnay |
| 4 | Merlot |

That answers our question, and it isn't too much trouble to writ out each DrinkName when we only have three different wines. But if we had a huge wine list, typing in each of them would be ridiculously dull. What's more, we'd have to updat the query every time we added a new wine to the menu.

There's a much easier way to do this. That first query we ran, the one which gave us the wine names, can give *SQL* the information it needs, too!

By using the wine-names-query as a **subquery**, we can feed that same data directly to SQL. All we need is a pair of parentheses. Then we can stick our first query into the second query in place of the list of wine names.

Here's how:

```
      SELECT COUNT(DrinkOrders.DrinkID) AS
NumDrinksSold, Menu.DrinkName
      FROM DrinkOrders
      JOIN Menu
      ON DrinkOrders.DrinkID = Menu.DrinkID
      WHERE DrinkOrders.DrinkID IN
          (SELECT Menu.DrinkID
          FROM Menu
          JOIN DrinkType
          ON Menu.DrinkTypeID =
DrinkType.DrinkTypeID
          WHERE  DrinkType.DrinkTypeName = 'Wine
      GROUP BY Menu.DrinkName
```

Results:

| NumDrinksSold | DrinkName |
|---|---|
| 2 | Cabernet |
| 4 | Chardonnay |
| 4 | Merlot |

There you go! We've saved ourselves some typing, and now if our menu changes, we won't have to re-write our query - any new wines will be automatically included.

One Important thing to note here - in the first line of our WHERE clause, we're using the keyword 'IN'. **If you're comparing multiple values in your WHERE clause, 'IN' must be used** instead of '='. If we used

```
...
WHERE Menu.DrinkID =
    (SELECT Menu.DrinkID
...
```

...we'd get an error.

## bqueries Vs. JOINs

Interestingly, you can often re-write subqueries into a single SELECT statement. How? Well, when you write a subquery, you're basically *making a virtual table*. SQL treats the output of the subquery as if it were another table in the database.

This query is functionally the same as the subquery one we just wrote:

```
    SELECT COUNT(DrinkOrders.DrinkID) AS
ımDrinksSold, Menu.DrinkName
    FROM DrinkOrders
    JOIN Menu ON DrinkOrders.DrinkID =
ınu.DrinkID
    JOIN DrinkType ON Menu.DrinkTypeID =
:inkType.DrinkTypeID
    WHERE DrinkType.DrinkTypeName = 'Wine'
    GROUP BY Menu.DrinkName
```

Results:

| NumDrinksSold | DrinkName |
|---:|---|
| 2 | Cabernet |
| 4 | Chardonnay |
| 4 | Merlot |

Here, we've used two JOINs in a row to get all of our data together. In SQL, you can JOIN as many tables together as you want - there is no limit. As long as the tables have a relationship, you can keep adding table after table to your query in a big table conga line to get all the data you need.

So, why not just stick with JOINs for everything, then? Well, subqueries can be easier to 'read' in a lot of cases. When other people look at your query (or when you come back to your own work weeks or months later), it can be easier to see what's going on if you have things broken out into different subqueries.

And sometimes you really just *need* a subquery to implement the logic you want. Remember the query we used in the previous chapter to find the most expensive drink?:

```
    SELECT TOP 1 DrinkName, DrinkID, DrinkPrice A
Most_Expensive_Drink
    FROM Menu
    ORDER BY DrinkPrice DESC
```

Using that as a subquery, we can find out how many sales there are for the most expensive drink:

```
      SELECT COUNT(DrinkOrders.DrinkID) AS
:pensiveDrinksSold, Menu.DrinkName
      FROM DrinkOrders
      JOIN Menu ON DrinkOrders.DrinkID =
:nu.DrinkID
      WHERE Menu.DrinkID =
          (SELECT TOP 1 DrinkID AS
·st_Expensive_Drink
          FROM Menu
          ORDER BY DrinkPrice DESC)
      GROUP BY Menu.DrinkName
```

esults:

| pensiveDrinksSold | DrinkName |
|---|---|
| 4 | Merlot |

You couldn't do that with a simple JOIN. Since you need the logic that finds the TOP 1 record, a subquery is the way to go.

Why do subqueries work? Well, SQL is all about **sets**. When you write a SQL query, you're asking the database to produce a **dataset** - essentially, a spreadsheet-like collection of rows and columns full of all the data that matches your query's criteria. A dataset can be of any size, from nothing at all (an 'empty dataset') to a single cell, or hundreds of columns and millions of rows.

Tables are basically permanent datasets. **Since every query produces a dataset, you can use any SQL query as if it were a table**. Subqueries can be JOINed, used in WHERE clauses, and more.

One quick note for programmers - if you're used to object-oriented programming languages, thinking in sets ca take some getting used to. In a language like Java or C#, you would likely answer the question of which drinks sold tl best by iterating over the DrinkOrders table one row at a time, looking up other data and applying filters until you've found the right information. **Don't do that with SQL -** working one row at a time is hugely slow and inefficient her Let SQL do all the heavy lifting for you by just pointing it at the tables you want, and letting it handle the rest. It's just a matter of telling it what you want it to do, not how to do it.

*Chapter 6*

# How to Read Someone Else's Query

*Welcome to the team! It's your turn to try to understand what the previous guy did.*

s pretty much inevitable - before too long, you're going to be sked to make a change to an existing query, or to find out what's rong with the code someone else wrote.

'hen faced with a whole bunch of SQL code that you've never en before, where do you even begin? How can you translate it to something you can understand?

can be easy to get lost inside someone else's badly-written query, here's a five-step checklist to keep you on track:

**T**our the tables
**W**ork from within
**F**igure out the filters
**L**ook over the logic
**C**onsider the comments

hile it doesn't spell anything catchy, you can remember TWFLC "Technical Work Fills Lonely Computers", if that helps.

SQL With a Sr

Let's put these five steps into action. Here's a nice, big query we can use as our sample:

```
      SELECT DD.CalendarYear, DD.DateID,
SUM(FACT.MetricValue) AS MetricValue,
DM.MetricName, TR.Threshold1, TR.Threshold2 FROM
FactTable FACT INNER JOIN DimMetric DM ON DM.Metric
= FACT.MetricID INNER JOIN dbo.DimDate DD ON
DD.DateID = FACT.DateID INNER JOIN (SELECT DISTIN
DD.DateID, TARG.MetricID, TARG.Threshold1,
TARG.Threshold2 FROM dbo.FactTarget TARG LEFT OUT
JOIN DimDate DD ON DD.WeekOfYear = TARG.WeekOfYe
AND DD.DayOfWeek = TARG.DayOfWeek) TR ON TR.DateI
DD.DateID AND TR.MetricID = FACT.MetricID WHERE
DD.CalendarYear = 2016 GROUP BY DD.CalendarYear,
DD.DateID, DM.MetricName, TR.Threshold1,
TR.Threshold2 ORDER BY DateID ASC
```

Holy guacamole, that's quite the wall of text! What a mess.

Before we can dive into the five steps outlined above, let's get this query in order. It will be a lot easier to work with once we've fixed the formatting.

While I'd hope that no human developer would write a query so messily, it's very common to see something like this if you're working with auto-generated code.

SQL ignores all blank spaces between keywords when processing a query, so it's not a problem for the computer to understand this mess. But since that's nearly impossible to read, we might as well put in some spaces and line-breaks so we poor humans have a chance of comprehending it.

Start by locating each of the clauses and main functions in the query. Most SQL programs will highlight keywords like SELECT, FROM, JOIN, and GROUP BY for you, so they're pretty easy to spot. Wherever you see one of those keywords, move it onto a ne line:

71

```
    SELECT DD.CalendarYear,
).DateID,SUM(FACT.MetricValue) AS MetricValue,
1.MetricName, TR.Threshold1, TR.Threshold2
    FROM FactTable FACT
    INNER JOIN DimMetric DM
    ON DM.MetricID = FACT.MetricID
    INNER JOIN dbo.DimDate DD ON DD.DateID =
\CT.DateID
    INNER JOIN (
    SELECT DISTINCT DD.DateID, TARG.MetricID,
\RG.Threshold1, TARG.Threshold2
    FROM dbo.FactTarget TARG
    LEFT OUTER JOIN DimDate DD ON DD.WeekOfYear =
\RG.WeekOfYear
    AND DD.DayOfWeek = TARG.DayOfWeek) TR ON
\.DateID = DD.DateID
    AND TR.MetricID = FACT.MetricID
    WHERE DD.CalendarYear = 2016
    GROUP BY DD.CalendarYear, DD.DateID,
1.MetricName, TR.Threshold1, TR.Threshold2
    ORDER BY DateID ASC
```

ιat's looking a bit better already.

e can make this even neater, but exactly what you want to do
ιm here depends on the conventions of your workplace and your
rsonal style.

ke to break out each item in the SELECT clause onto its own
e, keeping the comma at the beginning of the line. It does look
ιird, and at first I resisted doing this - but it actually helps a lot if
u need to go back and remove something later. It's also
ηsidered a 'best practice' with teams at some big Pacific
ιrthwest software companies.

ιre's how that looks:

```
      SELECT DD.CalendarYear
    , DD.DateID
    , SUM(FACT.MetricValue) AS MetricValue
    , DM.MetricName
    , TR.Threshold1
    , TR.Threshold2

      FROM FactTable FACT
      INNER JOIN DimMetric DM ON DM.MetricID =
FACT.MetricID
      INNER JOIN dbo.DimDate DD ON DD.DateID =
FACT.DateID
      INNER JOIN (
      SELECT DISTINCT DD.DateID
    , TARG.MetricID
    , TARG.Threshold1
    , TARG.Threshold2
      FROM dbo.FactTarget TARG
      LEFT OUTER JOIN DimDate DD ON DD.WeekOfYear
TARG.WeekOfYear
      AND DD.DayOfWeek = TARG.DayOfWeek
    ) TR ON TR.DateID = DD.DateID
      AND TR.MetricID = FACT.MetricID

      WHERE DD.CalendarYear = 2016

      GROUP BY DD.CalendarYear
    , DD.DateID
    , DM.MetricName
    , TR.Threshold1
    , TR.Threshold2

      ORDER BY DateID ASC
```

That's getting pretty read-able now! You can see now that there is
sub-query in this example, hiding in the outer query's FROM
clause. To make that easier to read, I like to indent the subquery,
and move each 'ON' statement to a separate line:

```
SELECT DD.CalendarYear
,DD.DateID
,SUM(FACT.MetricValue) AS MetricValue
,DM.MetricName
,TR.Threshold1
,TR.Threshold2

FROM FactTable FACT
INNER JOIN DimMetric DM
ON DM.MetricID = FACT.MetricID
INNER JOIN dbo.DimDate DD
ON DD.DateID = FACT.DateID
INNER JOIN
    (
        SELECT DISTINCT DD.DateID
        ,TARG.MetricID
        ,TARG.Threshold1
        ,TARG.Threshold2
        FROM dbo.FactTarget TARG
        LEFT OUTER JOIN DimDate DD
        ON DD.WeekOfYear = TARG.WeekOfYear
        AND DD.DayOfWeek = TARG.DayOfWeek
    ) TR ON TR.DateID = DD.DateID
    AND TR.MetricID = FACT.MetricID

WHERE DD.CalendarYear = 2016

GROUP BY DD.CalendarYear
,DD.DateID
,DM.MetricName
,TR.Threshold1
,TR.Threshold2

ORDER BY DateID ASC
```

hh, at last, our query is pretty and easy to read.
d man, there's a lot going on there! Don't worry though, it's
thing we haven't seen already.
t's go through that checklist one step at a time.

## Step 1) Tour the tables
First of all, let's find all of the tables used in the query.
In the outer query, we've got:
*FactTable FACT*
*DimMetric DM*
*DimDate DD*

And in the subquery:
*FactTarget TARG*
*DimDate DD*

That makes four tables total, since one of them, DimDate, appea twice.

Let's go through each of them:

**FactTable** - **Fact tables** are the star of the show. A fact table contains the measures you'll be reporting on - things like *sales*, *profit*, or *quantity sold*. Fact tables are where all the important numbers come from, and the figures you'll add up to see how the organization is performing.
In our earlier examples, DrinkOrders was the fact table, since we used it to count up how many orders were placed and how many drinks were sold.

**FactTarget** - In a lot of business applications, you'll have a **targe** or **goal** value - for example, 1 million pageviews, or 20% more items sold this year vs. last year. In this example, these values are stored in a table. In real life, these may be in a table, hard-coded into a report, or calculated based on prior performance.

**DimMetric** - Here, "Dim" is short for Dimension. **Dimension table** *describe* the facts. Rather than storing the important numbers themselves, dimension tables store information *about* those numbers.
In our earlier examples, DrinkType was a dimension table, since it told us *about* the drinks that were sold.

**mDate** - **Date dimensions** are an extremely common kind of ole. They let you group and filter the facts more easily - so you n report all sales for the month, or compare the quantity sold for ay of this year against May the prior year.

you weren't already familiar with these tables, you would probably ant to run a couple of quick queries to get to know the data. You uld try running queries such as

```
SELECT TOP 10 *
FROM FactTable
```

```
SELECT COUNT(*)
FROM DimMetric
```

To get a look at the sort of information you're working with, and w large each table is.

### ep 2) Work from within

right, now that we have a basic idea of what data we're working th, let's see what's being done with it. Let's work from the inside t to start figuring out what's going on here.

nce SQL parses inner queries first, it makes sense for us to take ook at those first as well. And we do have a subquery here, in the ROM clause:

```
INNER JOIN
    (
        SELECT DISTINCT DD.DateID
        ,TARG.MetricID
        ,TARG.Threshold1
        ,TARG.Threshold2
        FROM dbo.FactTarget TARG
        LEFT OUTER JOIN DimDate DD
        ON DD.WeekOfYear = TARG.WeekOfYea
        AND DD.DayOfWeek = TARG.DayOfWeek
    ) TR ON TR.DateID = DD.DateID
    AND TR.MetricID = FACT.MetricID
```

Take a look at the SELECT clause to see what data is being pull
for the subquery. We're getting a date identifier, a metric identifie
and some target values.

See that ON clause? The date and metric identifiers are used to
relate the tables DimDate and FactTable.

So this subquery is pulling back **target values** for our **metrics**, b
**date**.

One more thing to note - we can see that this subquery has the
alias TR, so we know that any fields called *TR.Something* in the
outer SELECT clause must come from this subquery.

### Step 3) Figure out the filters

It's time to check out the WHERE clauses. There's no WHERE
clause in our subquery, but there is one in the outer query:

```
WHERE DD.CalendarYear = 2016
```

Pretty straightforward - we're looking for **values from the calend**
**year 2016**.

Remember, though, that this isn't the only way filters can be

lied. **The act of JOINing tables together can filter your
ults**, as we saw in the Venn diagrams back in chapter 2. Take a
c at the FROM clause in the outer query:

```
FROM FactTable FACT
INNER JOIN DimMetric DM
ON DM.MetricID = FACT.MetricID
INNER JOIN dbo.DimDate DD
ON DD.DateID = FACT.DateID
INNER JOIN
    (
        SELECT DISTINCT DD.DateID
        , TARG.MetricID
        , TARG.Threshold1
        , TARG.Threshold2
        FROM dbo.FactTarget TARG
        LEFT OUTER JOIN DimDate DD
        ON DD.WeekOfYear = TARG.WeekOfYear
        AND DD.DayOfWeek = TARG.DayOfWeek
    ) TR ON TR.DateID = DD.DateID
    AND TR.MetricID = FACT.MetricID
```

ere are three INNER JOINs there. That means that **our data has
appear in each and every one of those tables, or it won't end
in our result set**. If any one of those tables is missing some
a, we won't be getting any rows back for that metric. If a metric
esn't have a date associated with it, for example, it wouldn't
ow up in our results.

ou were troubleshooting this query, this is a good place to pause
d spend some time putting everything together. If someone had
ced you to look at this query because a metric was missing from
eport, for example, you'd want to take a look at anything that
ght filter the data. You might need to:

- Change the CalendarYear filter in the WHERE clause
- Change the three INNER JOINs to OUTER JOINs to make
  sure all the values you wanted were returned
  - For example, if someone had forgotten to enter a

record in the DimDate table for a particular DateID, the fact that an INNER JOIN is used to connect FactTable and DimDate means that we wouldn't ge any data back

- Check for problems with the data in each table

## *Step 4) Look over the logic*

Alright, we've got a basic idea of where the data's coming from, what kind of data we're dealing with, and how it's being filtered. Now we can look at the **SELECT**, **ORDER BY**, and **GROUP BY** clause(s) to see **what's being done with it**.

Let's start with the SELECT clause from the outer query:

```
SELECT DD.CalendarYear
,DD.DateID
,SUM(FACT.MetricValue) AS MetricValue
,DM.MetricName
,TR.Threshold1
,TR.Threshold2
```

We already know that the TR.Threshold values are coming from our subquery, since our subquery is called TR. We've also got ye date, and metric name fields.

There's only one value being aggregated - *MetricValue*, which comes from our fact table. Since MetricValue is being aggregatec we know it won't show up in our GROUP BY.

Speaking of the GROUP BY, let's take a look at the end of the query:

```
GROUP BY DD.CalendarYear
,DD.DateID
,DM.MetricName
,TR.Threshold1
,TR.Threshold2
ORDER BY DateID ASC
```

etty straightforward - we've got all the expected values there.

e can also see that our ORDER BY is sorting by date. Since we
n't have a TOP clause, all that ORDER BY clause does is
range things by date in our final output.

## ep 5) Consider the comments

ere's one thing this query is missing completely - comments!

 in other programming languages, you can enter notes anywhere
your SQL code to help yourself and others figure out what's
ing on.

etty much anyone who has ever written a line of code will have
 opinion on when and where comments are needed, but in
neral, it's good to add them **wherever things might be unclear**
**someone else came and looked at your code**. When in doubt,
r on the side of entering **more** comments, not less. You never
ow what might help someone else down the line!

ere are two different ways to put comments in SQL code. To
ter a single-line comment, you can use two dashes

```
--Like this
```

.Or you can enclose your comments in slashes and asterisks, to
mment on multiple lines

```
/*Like
This.*/
```

 good to get into the habit of entering comments wherever
u've done something tricky, or (if you're reviewing someone
se's code), wherever it took you a while to figure a part of it out.

me teams will also ask you to add some comments about who

wrote the code and when, or what software uses the data from the query. It's a good idea to check with teammates to see if there are any conventions they'd like you to follow.

Here's how our sample query might look after we've added some comments:

```
/*
Used for: Executive Metric Dashboard
Created by: Joe Green, 1/1/2016
Modified by: Julie Smith, 1/15/2016
*/
SELECT DD.CalendarYear
,DD.DateID
,SUM(FACT.MetricValue) AS MetricValue
,DM.MetricName
,TR.Threshold1
,TR.Threshold2

FROM FactTable FACT
INNER JOIN DimMetric DM
ON DM.MetricID = FACT.MetricID
INNER JOIN dbo.DimDate DD
ON DD.DateID = FACT.DateID
INNER JOIN
        --Subquery to obtain threshold targets
        (
                SELECT DISTINCT DD.DateID
                ,TARG.MetricID
                ,TARG.Threshold1
                ,TARG.Threshold2
                FROM dbo.FactTarget TARG
                LEFT OUTER JOIN DimDate DD
                ON DD.WeekOfYear = TARG.WeekOfYea
                AND DD.DayOfWeek = TARG.DayOfWeek
        ) TR ON TR.DateID = DD.DateID
        AND TR.MetricID = FACT.MetricID
--2016 Only
WHERE DD.CalendarYear = 2016
```

```
GROUP BY DD.CalendarYear
,DD.DateID
,DM.MetricName
,TR.Threshold1
,TR.Threshold2

--Sorting by date for the report
ORDER BY DateID ASC
```

ow you can see why we've moved those commas to the
ginning of each line. If you decide that you don't want to include
e of those fields, you can quickly comment it out without affecting
e rest of the query:

```
SELECT DD.CalendarYear
--,DD.DateID
,SUM(FACT.MetricValue) AS MetricValue
,DM.MetricName
,TR.Threshold1
--,TR.Threshold2
```

d that's it! We've parsed the whole query. We've even added
me useful comments, so anyone else who looks at it will be able
figure it out even faster than we did.

ading a query is all about reverse-engineering the original
estion. By putting together the information we gathered from
ch step, we can now translate this query as:

*ve me metric information, including thresholds, dates, and the*
*etric name, for all metrics that have a valid threshold target during*
*e calendar year 2016.*

# *Conclusion*

You've made it! Congratulations!
Now you've got the basics down, and you can:
- Identify the main parts (clauses) of a SQL query
- Join tables
- Filter results
- Apply aggregate functions
- Make your own Top 10 lists
- Write subqueries
- And even read other people's queries, no matter how horrible they may be.

With all that, you're ready to start developing your own SQL code!

As you've seen, learning to write SQL is just a matter of **identifying the question you want to ask, and phrasing it in a way the SQL database can understand**.

In fact, it's just like learning a foreign language. What you've just learned is the equivalent of a first-year language course. It'll get you by if you're just visiting, but if you'll be living in database country for a while, you'll eventually find that you want to ask SQL a question that you don't have the words for. That's when you'll want to pick up some new functions and concepts. The wonderful thing about working with SQL is that **you don't have to learn it all at once** for it to be useful. You have the skills you need *right now* to write valuable queries that will give you useful information.

While this book may be all you ever need if you're just visiting the world of SQL, you can choose at any time to dive deeper and start learning more cool tricks. If you find you're using SQL to get chunks of data and then spending hours manipulating the results in your program or an Excel spreadsheet, look around and see if there's a way SQL can save you time. I bet it can.

The more SQL you know, the more you can make it do the wo *for* you. And the more you do inside your query, the faster things go. Remember, SQL is all about saving yourself time by making the *computer* do all the work.

So get out there, write some SQL code, and keep learning!

# *About the Author*

Elaine Kellner is a SQL developer and Business Intelligence ru with a taste for good beer and bad jokes.

After colliding headfirst into SQL while on the job, she found rself in a whirlwind workplace romance with databases. Now, she ints to share her love of SQL (and a few bad puns) with you.

In this introductory book, Elaine shows readers the basics of ading and writing SQL code, and shares practical, real-life advice m her years at large Pacific Northwest software companies.

21386674R00054

Printed in Great Britain
by Amazon